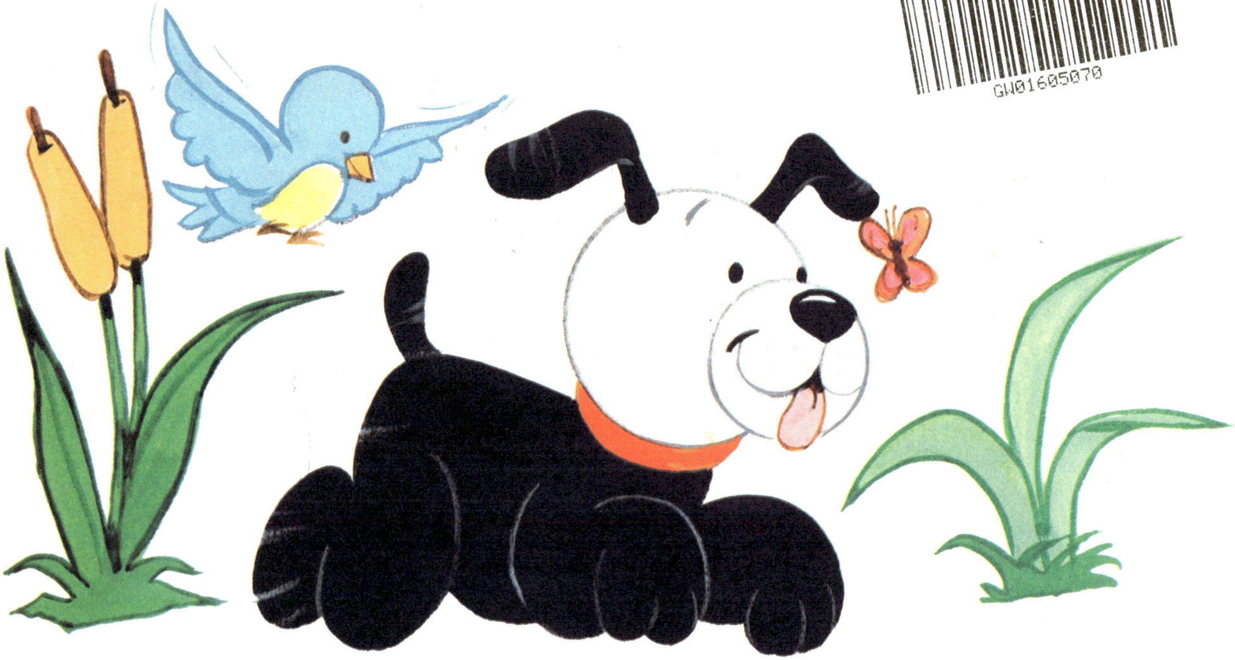

Lucky and the Dog Show

by Jon Chardiet • illustrated by Manny Campana

 Programme created by Parachute Press, Inc. Published by Marvel Books, 23 Redan Place, London W2.

Printed in Italy ISBN 0-948936-74-6

One spring day, Penny and Timmy were taking Lucky for a walk when they saw a sign on a tree.

"Wow!" said Penny. "We can enter Lucky for the dog show and win a prize."

"Not a chance," Timmy said. "Roger Goodwin's dog, Hero, is sure to win."

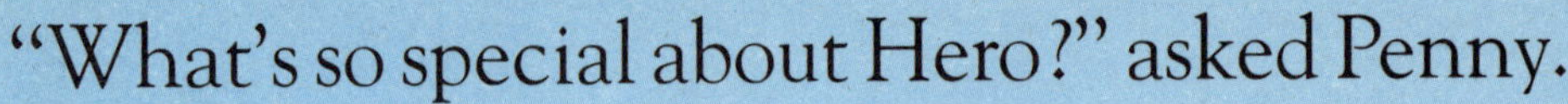

"What's so special about Hero?" asked Penny.

"Well, to begin with," said Timmy, 'Hero can jump through a hoop, balance a ball on his nose, ride a bike, and stand upside down on his two front paws. That's not all! Hero can sit in a chair. . . turn on the TV, carry dinner on his back, and dance while Roger plays the tin whistle."

"Lucky can't even roll over and play dead," said Timmy. "He can't even fetch the newspaper."

Lucky seemed to know they were talking about him. He ran over and licked Timmy's face.

"Oh, Lucky! Stop it, you silly dog," laughed Timmy.

Just then Roger Goodwin and Hero came running down the street.

"Hey, Timmy," shouted Roger. "I've just taught Hero a new trick. Want to see it?"

Roger snapped his fingers. Hero took a running jump and landed on Roger's shoulders.

“Wow! That’s a great trick, Roger,” said Timmy.

“It’s nothing,” said Roger. “By the way, is that your dog?” he asked, pointing to Lucky.

“Yes,” said Timmy in a quiet voice.

“What’s his name, Mucky?” Roger giggled.

Hero barked proudly. Poor Lucky! He looked so embarrassed!

Suddenly, Penny blurted out, "His name is Lucky and he's the best dog in the whole world. Lucky knows a hundred more tricks than your old Hero. And Lucky is going to win the dog show this year."

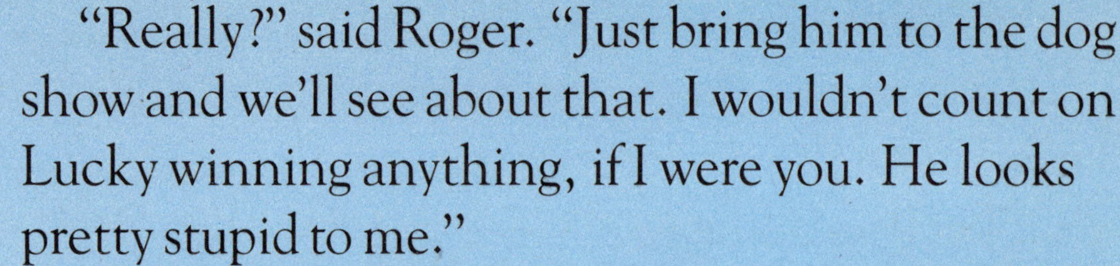

"Really?" said Roger. "Just bring him to the dog show and we'll see about that. I wouldn't count on Lucky winning anything, if I were you. He looks pretty stupid to me."

And with that, Roger and Hero ran off down the road.

"What are we going to do now?" asked Timmy.

"We're going to teach Lucky to do all of those tricks," said Penny. "And we're going to win the show."

"Arf!" said Lucky.

The next day after school, Lucky's training began. "Here, Lucky," said Timmy. "Jump through the hoop."

But all Lucky did was bite the hoop and pull on it. Then Penny threw a ball and said, "Lucky, fetch." Lucky ran for the ball, but then he ran off and hid it in the bushes.

After ten tries, Penny said, "I give up."

"Let's teach him something simple, like sit and stay," said Penny.

"Sit," said Timmy. Lucky actually sat.

"That's a good dog," said Timmy. "Now stay."

Lucky stayed...until he spotted a cat.

"Oh, no!" Timmy cried as Lucky knocked him over. "It's no use. Lucky will never learn to do tricks by Saturday."

Lucky ran to Penny and licked her face. Penny gave Lucky a hug. "I don't care if you don't know any tricks," she said. "You're still the best dog in the whole world."

"You're right," said Timmy. "There's no dog like Lucky."

The Saturday morning of the dog show, Penny came up with an idea. "If Lucky can't win a prize for doing tricks, he can surely win for being the best looking dog. Let's give Lucky a bath, right now."

When Lucky heard the word BATH, he started to run away.

But Timmy and Penny were too fast for him. Soon Lucky was nipping at the sponge and barking at the soap bubbles.

“Sit still,” said Penny as she dried and brushed Lucky. Then she tied big bows around his neck, ears, tail, and legs.

“What a beauty,” said Penny. “Now I’m sure you’ll win the prize.”

“I think he looks silly,” said Timmy.

Soon afterwards, Penny and Timmy left for the big hill in the park where the dog show was taking place. Everyone was lining up their dogs for the first event—a dog race.

"On your marks. . . get set. . . go!" shouted the official. All the dogs started running – all, except for Lucky.

"Where is he?" asked Penny.

"Where is he?" asked Timmy.

"He's running the wrong way," said Roger.

The next event was the ball fetch. Lucky was the first one up.

"Lucky, please go for the ball," whispered Timmy as he threw the ball high in the air.

"Look!" shouted Penny. "Lucky's running after it. He's got it. Hooray!"

All of a sudden, everyone started laughing.
"What's going on?" asked Penny.
"Don't look now, but *your* dog is burying the ball," said Timmy.

Then it was time for the obedience test. Roger and Hero were called up first. Hero, of course, did everything right. He sat. He stayed. He came on command.

"Hero's score is 100," said the judge.

Then Penny, Timmy, and Lucky were called.
"Lucky, sit!" said Timmy.
Lucky lay down and played dead.
"Lucky, come!" said Penny.
Lucky sat.
"Lucky, roll over," said Timmy.

Lucky ran up and licked Timmy's face. Everyone was laughing...except Timmy and Penny.

"Roll over," shouted Timmy. This time Lucky did. He rolled over and over and over...all the way down the big hill.

The other dogs must have thought Lucky was having fun. Pam Carpenter's dog rolled down the hill, just like Lucky. Then one by one the other dogs followed...except for Hero who stayed by Roger's side.

“It’s time for the decoy duck race,” said the official. “Each dog in turn must swim to the middle of the lake and bring back the wooden duck.”

Hero was called up first. No other dog could swim as fast as he could. Roger was certain that Hero would win. Everyone gathered around the lake to watch.

Hero swam towards the duck.
"He's got the duck," shouted Roger.
But suddenly, Hero disappeared under the water.
"Oh, no!" Roger cried. "Hero must have a cramp. I'll never reach him in time. Someone, please help!"

Like a flash, before anyone could make a move, Lucky dived into the water. Everyone stood and watched silently.

Then Timmy yelled, “Look, Lucky’s got Hero. He’s pulling him to shore.”

Everyone cheered!

"Well," said the judge as he finished giving out most of the awards, "Now it's time for the grand prize. This is for the best dog in the neighbourhood. If you all agree, I think Lucky deserves it for his bravery."

Everyone shouted, "Hooray, hooray!" – even Roger Goodwin.